Stanley Leathes

The Claims of the Old Testament

Stanley Leathes

The Claims of the Old Testament

ISBN/EAN: 9783337169435

Printed in Europe, USA, Canada, Australia, Japan

Cover: Foto ©Lupo / pixelio.de

More available books at **www.hansebooks.com**

THE

CLAIMS OF THE OLD TESTAMENT

LECTURES DELIVERED IN CONNECTION WITH
THE SESQUICENTENNIAL CELEBRATION
OF PRINCETON UNIVERSITY

BY

STANLEY LEATHES, D.D.

PROFESSOR OF OLD TESTAMENT EXEGESIS
IN KING'S COLLEGE, LONDON

NEW YORK
CHARLES SCRIBNER'S SONS
1897

University Press:

JOHN WILSON AND SON, CAMBRIDGE, U.S.A.

THE CLAIMS OF THE OLD TESTAMENT

LECTURE 1

In the two lectures I shall have the honor to give in response to your kind invitation, I shall endeavor to investigate the reasons for which we accept the Old Testament as the record of a revelation possessed of Divine authority, and inquire how far they are affected by recent theories and speculations concerning it. There would seem at first sight to be something of the nature of surprise in the fact that a tradition which has held its ground for at least two thousand years, and is common alike to the antagonistic Jewish and Christian churches, should be found at last delusive and erroneous ostensibly on the ground of scholarship, though accepted and handed down by some of the greatest of scholars from the first; and this with so much of confidence and assurance that to offer any apology for a tradition so venerable is to incur forthwith the re-

proach of being no scholar, and to be pronounced
disqualified for forming or uttering any opinion
on the matter; though at the same time it must
persistently be borne in mind that it was em-
phatically declared by the pioneers of the anti-
traditional views that the question raised was
not one of scholarship at all, but much rather
of ordinary judgment and common-sense, such
as any intelligent man might be supposed to possess. "The critic," we are told by Kuenen, "has
no other Bible than the public. He does not
profess to have any additional documents inac-
cessible to the laity, nor does he profess to find
anything in his Bible that the ordinary reader
cannot see." This is sufficiently precise and clear,
and it must not be forgotten in the course of
discussion.

There is, however, surely an element of weakness betrayed by the fact that notwithstanding
the bar of common-sense is thus so frankly appealed to, no sooner does a layman, or a divine of
the traditional school, engage in the controversy
than he is at once silenced by the cry, "Oh,
but you are no scholar. Without the profound
grammatical and linguistic knowledge of an expert, and without having the visual ray purged
so as to be enabled to recognize the broad and

patent characteristics that distinguish the several contributions of J. and E. and D. and P. and Q. and R., you are of course not capable of appreciating the irrefragable character of the verdict given by those who are, nor of seeing how absolutely certain and conclusive it is." Now, it is this initial inconsistency of which I complain. Either the Bible is an open book or it is not. If it is, then my opinion, even as a layman, if I can substantiate it, may be as good as yours; and it is not I or you, but the unlearned public at large, who must judge. If the Bible is not an open book, then the matter must be left to scholars; but in that case what becomes of the boast of Kuenen, that the critic has no other Bible than the public; and what becomes of the court to which the appeal was so confidently and magnanimously made? There is a manifest inconsistency here, and it would seem as if the patent *volte face* which is so deftly executed argued some uncertainty about the actual premises which might not improbably vitiate the conclusions.

If there is really the manifest difference between the several component parts of Genesis, for example, declared to be visible to the critical eye, how is it that they are not more readily

discernible by the naked eye of the ordinary
reader? But must we not allow that the ordinary reader who will avail himself of Dr. Bis-
sell's " Genesis printed in Colors," will not only
be perplexed to distinguish the several sections,
but also receive the most demonstrative object-
lesson as to the worthlessness of the scholarship,
or at least the judgment, which can accept, as
valid, conclusions so preposterous? Is it possible to show a more demonstrative *reductio ad
absurdum* of the principles it is proposed to illustrate? Surely, if criticism can accept this without nausea, the taste of common-sense must be
fastidious indeed.

It is considerations such as these that lead us to
conclude that there must be some other principles
in operation that produce a result so clearly out
of harmony with the professions so loudly made.
If the Bible is the possession of every man, then
it has a message for every man, and every man is
capable of judging of the character and claims
of the message. But if the message of the Bible
is for the critic alone, then no one else needs to
trouble himself about it. But it is because the
Bible is largely felt to have a message for every
man, that we cannot calmly acquiesce in giving
it over to the critics.

Again, it must be borne in mind that it is with the Bible as with every other book; that the aspect it presents cannot but vary according as it is approached with trust or with suspicion. There is no document and no composition that is proof against unfavorable treatment; and if the Bible is read with the intention of discrediting it, there is no prerogative of immunity attaching to it which will avert the consequences.

And moreover it would seem to be unfair to allow the presence of the supernatural in the Old and New Testaments to prejudice the case against either, inasmuch as it is this which is the inherent and essential character of their message. They manifestly profess to come with a special message from God, and it is not on account of this profession that they are at once to be rejected; but it is hard to see how the reality of the message can be guaranteed except by the credentials which accompany it. The fact and significance of the supernatural in Scripture is the matter in dispute, and to decide beforehand that on this ground Scripture is to be rejected, is to beg an initial question that we have no right to grant. By all means let us treat Scripture fairly and criticise it freely, but let us not shut our eyes to those characteristics which differen-

tiate it from all other literature, and which therefore constitute part of its inalienable endowment,
and consequently go a long way towards estab-
lishing its claim. To enter on the discussion
with a bias against the main position of Scripture is to render ourselves unfit to conduct it.

And having said thus much, I proceed to ask
what the Old Testament is, and what its claims
are upon our attention. Now, the Old Testament, or the Old Covenant, as it ought to be called,
in its name implies two things: first, that it is
the record of a covenant with God; and secondly,
that it is old, with respect to one that is newer.
And these two points involve the whole case
with reference to the Old Testament. For they
imply that God was the author of the covenant
recorded, and that this covenant was after all
only preparatory to another; that it was therefore incomplete and (imperfect,) but nevertheless
possessed the virtual promise of another. And it
is here that very important issues are involved;
because the very conception of God's making a
covenant with any person or people implies a
conception of God and His method of operation
entirely distinct from and contrary to anything
we can learn of God in nature. Nature and her
operations are indifferent and universal. She

treats all alike. The very conception of God's making a covenant with any person or people implies selection, favoritism, exemption ; the very antithesis of the universal and the indiscriminate. And therefore here, apart altogether from any supernatural exhibition of power or action, there is involved a thought which is antagonistic to anything that nature as the administrator of the universal has to teach us or can exhibit. It is impossible to conceive of God's making a covenant without supposing Him to come out of the darkness and obscurity with which He commonly shrouds Himself in order to enter into special relations with those to whom He thus exceptionally draws nigh. And this of itself, apart from anything else, involves the miraculous, the extraordinary, and the supernatural. To maintain, therefore, that on this account the record of such action is to be rejected is fatal to the entire professed revelation. We cannot deal with it without belying its essential character and credentials. And any further action toward it on our part is disingenuous and unfair. But then, secondly, if the sacred writings of the Jews contain the record of the old covenant of God, that of itself implies the fact that He has made a new one, and that the one was preparatory for the other. And as a

matter of fact the actual relation subsisting between the Old Testament and the New, will be
for all time the conclusive evidence of the reality
of the claims of both. It is simply impossible
to account for this relation in all its essential
features as a merely natural phenomenon and
without postulating a presiding, directing, and
designing agent who, independently of the various elements co-operating in its production, has
brought it about. Consequently, the book of
the old covenant bears its claim upon its surface,
and we cannot disguise the fact that we have to
deal with something that is of no ordinary character, and that makes no ordinary pretensions.
The book of the old covenant is nothing if it is
not a record of the various ways in which God
was pleased to deal with a particular nation for
the instruction and benefit of all, and with special
reference to His action in the future.

What, then, are some of the chief reasons on
account of which we are disposed to acknowledge the claims of the Old Testament upon our
regard? In the first place, there is the apparent
antiquity of its historical record. Whether this
is trustworthy or not, there is nothing in all literature to compare with it. Here we have a
bird's-eye view of human history from the very

first. Even if this is not as veracious as it seems to be, it is at least uncontradicted, original, and unique. There are no similar documents to call in question its statements, or to dispute its accuracy. We know absolutely nothing of the history of the race four thousand years ago, except what the Old Testament has recorded. The whole extent would be an absolute blank were it not for the light, such as it is, that is thrown upon it by the Old Testament. And against this we have nothing whatever to set but conjecture and uncertain inferences drawn from phenomena of uncertain import.

Again, there is the simplicity and comparative value of these early documents, when contrasted with such documents as we have of a like kind among other nations. Compare, for example, the cosmogonies of Hesiod or of Manu with those of Genesis, and we can but stand amazed at the simplicity and sublimity of the one, and the monstrosity, puerility, and absurdity of the other. In fact there is, and can be, no comparison. In the one case, we are dealing with apparent fact; in the other, with obvious conjecture and with patent falsehood. The first verse of the first chapter of Genesis tells us that which is antecedent to and independent of all science, which is rea-

sonable and probable in itself, which furnishes a
basis for all science, but is contradicted and re-
placed by none. We may well ask, then, On
whose authority is this stated? If it is false, can
we disprove it? If it is true, how did it enter into
the mind of the writer to utter and affirm it? If
it is true, how did it happen that he alone of all
men discovered its truth? For we cannot be
persuaded of its truth, unless there is authority
for believing it to be true; and the writer could
not give it any other authority than that on
which he, himself, received it. So that we may
state the matter thus. What is here told us is
either true or not true. If it is true we can only
know it to be true if it was divinely imparted;
otherwise it must be conjectural, and may or
may not be true. Now, as there is nothing to
contradict its truth, but very much to confirm it,
a strong presumption is created in favor of the
claim on its behalf; and certainly here alone,
among all statements and speculations of the
kind in ancient or in modern times, do we find
anything which speaks to us with so much of
the majesty of truth; which surely is no insignificant reason for believing it to be true, and
which is the more inconsistent with the supposition of its being false.

It is, however, only the few first chapters of Genesis which concern the race as a whole. As early as the twelfth chapter the horizon becomes contracted, and henceforth the fortunes of a single people only are related, great prominence being given to the history of the first father of the nation. It is here that we must determine the essential character of the narrative, because our decision about that will materially affect the judgment that we form of all that follows. The main question is whether it is myth or history; and how is this to be determined? I am not aware of any touchstone by which we can infallibly discern the one from the other, simply on internal and *à priori* principles. How do we know that Cæsar and Thucydides are true? How do we know that Hamlet and King Lear are not? Is it not a matter of evidence and traditional testimony in every case? And where there is room for doubt, how can the doubt be resolved but by the weighing of the evidence for and against? Now, there is absolutely no external evidence against the story of Abraham, — though we have been told by Butler, but often forget it, that there is a presumption of millions to one against the story of Cæsar or of any other man, — and it is only on internal prepossessions that this story can be rejected. But inasmuch as it professes to be the record of Divine manifestations, it is clearly not to be rejected on the ground that it professes to record them. And over and beyond this, the story of Abraham has this fact conspicuously in its favor, that it contains in germ the explanation of the subsequent national history, and is marvellously confirmed by the corroboration continuously afforded by that history up to the present day. Now, it is conceivable that a writer in the palmy days of the monarchy might have sought to illustrate the glory of the national throne by inventing a narrative like that of Abraham, surrounding it with an imaginary halo of romance and myth; but allowing the possibility of this, we are still at a loss to conceive any period of the national life at which the promise that all nations should be blessed in Abraham could have suggested itself to any mind or could have derived any corroboration from the actual or probable course of events. And yet here, on the forefront of this mythical history, we find this patent and daring challenge thrown down for posterity to verify or to discredit. And we may ask with confidence, What has the verdict been? And is not the marvellous correspondence between the promise and the facts of history some-

thing which defies explanation upon any natural
principles? And if so, is not this of itself the
highest testimony to the character of the original
narrative, and does it not create a distinct presumption in its favor? I do not see how we are
to explain the fact of this promise, many times
repeated in the Genesis history and referred to in
the subsequent[1] literature, but on the assumption that it was given under the circumstances
recorded; in which case we need hesitate no more
on account of any other supernatural incidents
by which it was accompanied. Indeed, any other
incidents of the kind can only be regarded as
tending to confirm the reality of the promise and
the facts of its divine origin.

And here perhaps it is right to say a word
about the much abused term "supernatural."
The Duke of Argyll, in his admirable book on the
"Philosophy of Belief," dwells upon the error of
distinguishing between the natural and the supernatural. But surely, however open to objection
scientifically this may be, confusion and misconception only can arise if we decline to distinguish
them. For instance, unless we use "nature" to
include not only the whole area of perceptive
knowledge and experience, but everything besides

---

[1] Micah vii. 20.

that is not "dreamt of in our philosophy," we must admit the distinction, however incorrect or misleading in the scientific sense it may be. For example, I suppose no one would affirm that the birth of Isaac, under the circumstances recorded, was a natural event or capable of natural explanation any more than the fact of the Lord's speaking to Abraham out of heaven was, however much we may choose to include both events under the term "natural," as embracing everything that has ever occurred. If this can rightly be done without impinging upon the historic truth of the narrative, well and good; but as I strongly suspect it cannot, then we must be very careful to contend for the facts recorded, whether we call them natural or supernatural. What I want to know is, did these two events ever take place? Does the narrative intend us to believe that they did? Is it right and true in that intention? and if it is, how far are we right in drawing the inference that they were intended to establish the reality of the divine communications given, and did establish it? And is there any other legitimate inference that we can draw? And the question herein involved is one that will perpetually confront us throughout the Scripture narrative, and therefore, sooner or later, we must deal with it;

for instance, if nowhere else, at least in the facts of our Lord's life. If that can be reduced to the dimensions of the natural, without any forfeiture of literal historic truth, then I am willing to surrender the *term* " supernatural "; but unless that can be done, no good will ensue from the desire to blink the necessity of using it, for we cannot afford to do so. And with regard to the like narratives of the Old Testament, either their historic veracity is a matter of no importance, or else their historic truth is absolutely discredited by the statements that involve the supernatural; for it is inconsistent to accept, for instance, the reality of the promise to Abraham, and reject the narrative concerning the birth of Isaac.

On the other hand, one is quite willing to admit that the acceptance of the supernatural in the narratives, for its own sake, is to stop short of the purpose for which it is narrated, which manifestly is with the intention of confirming the reality of the spiritual facts with which these narratives are associated, and which they illustrate. Take for example the narrative of the passage of the Jordan by the Israelites. I suppose no one will deny that that is related, and was always accepted, as a supernatural fact intended to confirm the promise of God, and to show forth

His special providence with regard to Israel. Now, the Duke of Argyll says that the Jordan ran dry in the thirteenth century of our era, owing to the falling of rock (p. 215), and uses that fact as an illustration of what may have taken place at the passage of the Israelites. But surely this is to deal unfairly with the Scripture narrative. Let it be granted that purely natural causes operated in both cases. Even then there are many circumstances in the Scripture narrative not explained: for instance, the statement of Joshua that within three days the host should pass over Jordan; that when the priests' feet touched the water the waters retreated and remained divided till all the host had passed over; and the like. If we accept the narrative at all, we must accept these facts; but if we accept these facts, and even suppose them to be susceptible of natural explanation, we have not explained the significance with which they were supposed to be fraught, and without which they were worthless in themselves, and productive only of error and misconception alike in the mind of the people and in that of the narrator. In short, this would be to suppose that the Almighty made use of delusion and deception, and that for the purpose of confirming the truth of His own

word. It seems to me, therefore, that, pare down
the supernatural as we may, and explain it as
only another phase of the natural, we must
eventually admit the reality of an essential difference between them, unless we are prepared to
reject the narratives; as, for example, in the ultimate instance, with the resurrection of Christ. ·
This either was or was not a literal fact; if it
was a literal fact, then it was in no ordinary
sense a natural one; if it was not a literal fact,
then we must reject the narrative, or are committed to the belief of a lie in accepting it. The
natural and the supernatural, therefore, as I take
it, are not synonymous. There may be a whole-
some dread of the marvellous for its own sake,
and a revulsion against supposing that, because
we do not stumble at the supernatural, therefore we are believers; but at the same time that
belief is not worthy of the name which insists
upon expunging every miracle and wonder alike
from the Christian creed and the Scripture record.
I do not understand how belief in any sense can
avoid being committed to the acceptance of certain facts which defy all natural explanation,
whether we call them miraculous, or spiritual, or
what not.

There is also another point in which a good

2

deal of loose thought appears to be current in the present day, and that is the essential connection between historic events and spiritual and moral truth. For example, it is asked, "What do we lose if Abraham, Isaac, and Jacob were mythical personages, with no historic existence? Do not the spiritual lessons remain which their narratives illustrate? The example of Abraham's faith abides, whether he is imaginary or real, just as the evil of marital jealousy remains whether Othello was, or was not, merely the creation of Shakespeare's brain." But this appears to me to betray a very unsatisfactory and vague conception of the necessary conditions of the problem to be solved. Let it be granted that the example of faith is the essential element in the story of Abraham; but let us also suppose that Abraham was a mythical personage, with no real existence. Then clearly the command which he obeyed and the promise which he believed were unreal too, as also was his obedience and his belief. Our position would then be this : "Had Abraham acted under the conditions supposed, as he is said to have acted, we have from the blessing promised upon his faith the corresponding advantage that may be expected to accrue to us from the like obedience and belief. The teaching of the narra-

tive is equally distinct and eloquent, whether
true or false." Very well; but if the narrative is
imaginary, so also may be the lessons derived from
it. We do not care to know what conceivably
might be the case under certain circumstances;
we want to know what actually was the case
under these circumstances as described. If God
did not act as He is said to have acted in the case
of Abraham, how do we know that He will act in
the like manner in our own case? What *proof*
have we that He cares at all about how we do
act? Because it must be borne in mind that if
the history of Abraham is dissipated in this way,
there is no reason why any other like narrative
may not be in like manner dissipated and destroyed. If the ground of faith is thus relegated
to the merely spiritual, impalpable, and intan-
gible, apart altogether from the concrete, visible
and substantial authority which vouches for it,
there ceases to be any valid foundation at all
for it, in the experimental and the real. Then
there is no necessity for God to confirm His word
with signs following, and in the great majority of
cases it is a mistake to suppose that He ever did.
Even in the time of Christ mankind had not
emerged from this pernicious and childish habit
of believing in signs, and in Old Testament times

they were immersed in it. For us there has been
reserved the far higher calling to dispense altogether with signs in the present, and to discredit
the reality of those which are said to have been
given in the past. *Faith*, if it is real, and in pro-
portion as it is, can dispense altogether with an
historic basis to rest on. There is no question
but that this is the direction in which men's
thoughts are largely moving. But is there not a
manifest and pernicious fallacy in the reasoning?
Because it is perfectly true that God would have
us be independent of signs, does He intend us to
believe that signs have never been given? Does
He wish us to suppose that those which are
alleged to have been given were fallacious, and
that it matters nothing whether they were real
or not? If so, surely not only the Old Testament,
but the New likewise must be written again
de novo. Then not only may we pass by the
miracles of Christ as of no moment, but we must
also believe that He never really wrought them,
and never actually appealed to them; that in all
these cases there was nothing more than tempo-
rary and apparent concession to human weakness.
But then, in that case, we must likewise deal in
some intelligible way with His birth, His life,
His resurrection, and His ascension.

It seems to me that the true point in which the purely spiritual and the real and actual meet, is the death of Christ. The solid ground on which faith rests as a sure foundation is the death of Christ. That death, regarded merely in its historic aspect in relation to the recorded acts and words of Jesus, points us unmistakably to something above and beyond nature, to something in the Divine, which speaks by it and yet differs from it, as Fatherhood differs from worship. And if this is so, then there is but one way of interpreting the darkness and the earth-quake; namely, as the recognition by the God of nature of the justice with which the sinless sufferer claimed to be the Son of God. Here we have most conspicuously the mingling of the natural and the supernatural; of that which was purely and simply human and ordinary with that which was essentially superhuman and miraculous, supernatural and divine.

But if you recognize the two elements here, is it only here that we may recognize them? And if it is, as I believe it to be, impossible not to recognize them here, may not the same be said with equal justice of many other events and incidents recorded alike in the Old Testament and the New? When, however, we have estab-

lished a firm foothold on the mere historic features and incidents of the death of Christ and
recognized that to which they unmistakably
point, it is not many steps further to lay equally
firm hold of the resurrection and ascension of
the Lord Jesus. When we have taken in the
full significance of the one, it is surely somewhat
less hard to see how naturally the one leads on
to the other, and the one is followed on and sup-
plemented by the other.

It is surely considerations such as these which
may serve to give us pause before we acquiesce
with too great facility in the opinion of those who
ask complacently, "What if, after all, it should
turn out that it has been part of God's plan in the
past to teach us by myth?" To which I would
reply by two other questions: What if it should,
after all, *not* turn out that such has been his plan?
And what about the death of Christ? Was
that a myth? Or is it a certain fact that the
mere naked historic incidents of that tremendous
act do point us unmistakably to further truths,
which would, however, most undeniably cease
to be true if the actuality of those incidents
could be called in question, — if, that is, they
themselves were mythical? So manifest is it
that those who recklessly use such language

with regard to the Old Testament have not
counted the cost of their too bland concessions,
and, what is more, have not fairly estimated the
essential foundations on which their own professed belief rests.   Before we are asked to admit
that it may be part of the Divine plan to teach
by myth, even as Christ taught by parables, let
us inquire the more earnestly what evidence there
is that He has done so, and let us not at once assume it, as a fact, merely because it falls in con-
veniently with certain theories which are absolutely fatal to the historic validity of the Old Testament as a whole.   Are we prepared to accept
the Old Testament as merely the story-book of
the Jewish race in its infancy, and to extract
from it only so much ethical wisdom as is consistent with our own preconceived and advanced
notions of what is wise and true; or are we willing to regard it rather as the record of special
Divine dealing with a race favored and chosen
for the express purpose of thereby teaching the
whole human family, and as revealing the foundations in history and literature upon which
God would afterwards erect the permanent edi-
fice of the Christian Church and build up the
temple of the kingdom of heaven?   For then,
manifestly, in whatever degree the Old Testa-

ment is this, it must stand to reason that we
cannot with equanimity regard those hypotheses
which assume, without proving, that these foundations are unstable and unsound, and would
thereby substitute a basis of lies for the substra-
tum of fact on which it claims to rest.

It seems to me that we cannot fairly understand the essential questions that underlie the
acceptance of the narratives of the Old Testament
and the New Testament alike without determin-
ing these two points: first, whether the ordinary laws of nature ever have historically been
infringed, violated, set aside, or what you will;
and secondly, whether this has ever been done for
the express purpose of accrediting the Divine
word and promises in a way that otherwise it
would seem impossible that they should be ac-
credited.   It is not the rejection of this or that
narrative in either volume of Scripture, but the
rejection of the whole tenor of Scripture through_
out from first to last, that alone is adequate, if
we are to answer these questions in the nega-
tive.   Christ undoubtedly appealed to His mighty
works in their physical as well as their moral
aspect, in confirmation of the claims He advanced.
Was He justified in doing this or not?   If He was,
did He not thereby virtually set His seal to the

principle that we are not wrong in believing that God's word may be confirmed by signs following?

And with regard to the limits of the natural and the supernatural, which it is so difficult to define, it must be borne in mind that a combination of purely natural incidents occurring naturally may be interpreted, and be meant to be interpreted, as giving Divine corroboration of a particular principle or course of action no less convincing and conclusive than the direct apparent suspension or infringement of known natural law would do. The question really at issue is, Under what conditions may we recognize the special declaration of the Divine will as intentionally communicated to us? Is it ever legitimate to do so, or is it mere superstition and self-deception in every case? If so, then it stands to reason that we must fling away the Bible as a worthless record; but if otherwise, then it may chance that there is no other record or collection of records so calculated and designed to direct us aright in this matter as are these. It is in that belief that I accept the New Testament and try to study the complex literature of the Old, as the divinely designed preparation for the more complete revelation which was to confirm and fulfil its promises and hopes.

Now, if the Bible is a layman's book, as it is alleged to be, it stands to reason that its defects or fallacies must be as patent to the layman as they are to the critic. But I, as a layman, want to learn whether I may frankly accept the Old Testament in its traditional character as a Divinely authorized narrative of the events it records, or must regard it as so modified and conditioned by traditional error and human mis-interpretation as to be utterly untrustworthy in its narrative of these events. The critic tells me explicitly that this is what he finds the Bible to be, and gives sundry reasons for it, which he says I, as a layman, am able to appreciate. But it so happens that, in a multitude of cases, I altogether dispute his conclusions and am wholly unconvinced by the reasons assigned. Of course neither he nor I am concerned to maintain the absolute inerrancy of every his-torical statement in the Old Testament, as, for example, the number and names of Esau's wives, and the like; but I do very much want to know whether, for example, the narrative of the first ten chapters of Exodus gives a correct or incor-rect account of the events recorded, whether the part ascribed to the Divine action is imaginary or real, whether the writer or the actor, *whoever he was*, exceeded his commission in appealing so confidently to the name of God. This is by no means a question merely of age and authorship, as regards the books, as Dr. Driver chooses to represent it (cf. Int. p. xix); it is simply a question of truth or falsehood; and I, as an interested layman, am determined to accept no middle position. Either it was God who brought Israel out of Egypt (Num. xxiii. 22), or that deliverance was an accidental escape with which the finger of God had nothing whatever to do, and which the historian therefore has entirely misrepresented. Now I want to know whether Moses and the Israelites had any more ground for recognizing the hand of God in their deliverance than Cromwell had in the battles of Dunbar and Worcester, — that is to say, does faith create its own basis of belief, or is there an external and objective ground on which it rests, which faith perceives and apprehends but does not create, and may we recognize in the Scripture narrative the voucher for such a ground, and find such an instance of it as we cannot find in the history of Cromwell? If we may, then have we in Scripture such a guaranteed objective ground of faith as we can rely on, and that because this its ordained function is not of man, but of God. But has the Scripture this function, and how do we know that it has it? Only because of its own inherent testimony to that effect, and of the credentials which it is able to present. But it stands to reason that unless the narrative of the exodus is ultimately from the chief personal actor in it, we cannot ascribe to it the authority requisite for its being trustworthy; and hence the inevitable consequence that if the narrative is five or six centuries after the period of the exodus, it cannot possibly serve as a voucher for the correctness of the statements it so daringly ascribes to God, but sinks to the level of Cromwell's belief about Dunbar and Worcester. It is to me a matter of simple astonishment that people do not see that unless we have an objective basis for faith, there is nothing for faith to rest on, and in this case such an objective basis cannot be given by an unknown and unauthorized narrative such as a work of the ninth century B.C. would necessarily be, but only by a narrative sufficiently expressing the declared word of God, and recording with sufficient accuracy the veritable acts of God.

And it has further to be borne in mind that in whatever way we conceive of a revelation being conveyed to man, such as that for example

of the Mosaic record of the exodus, two conditions would seem to be absolutely essential, —
namely, first, the accuracy of the recorded facts;
and, secondly, the attitude indispensable for
accepting them, which is one of faith. For suppose a revelation of plenary Divine authority
imparted to man, it must either be so given as
to compel acceptance, or it must be dependent on
the faith of man to be accepted. Now, no one
pretends that the supposed revelation of God is
a matter of demonstration; if it were, it would
not be possible to reject it, in which case it
would fail as a moral test; consequently, in
whatever way the revelation was presented it
would necessarily appeal to faith. Clearly, therefore, if the history of the exodus was intended
as a revelation of special Divine action and the
record of it, there would be the necessity not
only of its historic accuracy, but also for the
requisite disposition of mind to accept it. But if
its accuracy, not merely in detail, but in its
special characteristic as revealing the will and
working of God, were called in question, it would
fail altogether of its professedly designed result
as a revelation. But it is exactly this that is
called in question, if the form of the record is
five or six centuries after the time; and conse-

quently the ground of our belief in the narrative is absolutely destroyed, for we cannot be sure of the facts, and more especially of that fact which is the most important of all, namely, that the events recorded truly represent the operation of the Divine will. Not only are we uncertain as to what God said unto Moses, but we do not even know that He spake unto him at all, or that He was in any way to be identified with, or held responsible for, the course and tenor of the events. It is therefore all moonshine to say that if we destroy the " form " of the revelation, the " fact " remains untouched ;[1] because no fact at all remains, except so much as we choose to concede to popular prejudice, resting as it does in the mere word " revelation " without any specific authority whatever.

It is absolutely necessary that the critics should be " brought to book " in this respect, and be compelled to tell us what it is they really mean by revelation, and with what amount of belief in Holy Scripture their conclusions are ultimately compatible. They first of all dissipate *in toto* the traditional authority of the canon, whether it be in relation to the Pentateuch, Daniel, Joel, Jonah, or any other book contained therein, and show that

[1] See Driver, Int. p. xvi.

all such grounds of authority are purely imaginary; and having thereby demonstrated, as they suppose, the entirely untrustworthy character of the history and the external authority of the prophets, they continue to talk about revelation as if it were a thing that could float in the air without any foundation whatever to rest on. Having first entirely shattered the traditional authority of the word of God, they continue to speak of that word as though it could be not only independent of all external testimony, but was moreover a thing so evident and unquestionable in itself as to be able to laugh to scorn every critical result which was fatal to its received authority and to its traditional pretensions.

Let me make myself clearly understood. I place no barrier against criticism the most searching and impartial; by all means let us treat the Bible like any other book. I ask for no reservation in its favor; but, nevertheless, I feel most deeply that it is not on grounds such as those which the critics advance that the established position of the Bible is to be surrendered, even if it be that some of the traditional safeguards may be invalid, and that all may need modification and readjustment. I believe that many of the critical conclusions

are unsound, and that many more are unproven;
and I believe it to be wholly disingenuous and
unfair to affirm and reaffirm statements on the
authority of those conclusions which are in
themselves not only irreconcilable with Apos-
tolic affirmations, but also absolutely fatal to the
kind of substantial validity that is throughout
assumed for the Old Testament in the New.
And therefore it is wholly impossible to discuss
these questions as if nothing of any importance
depended on their issue; because the faith and
authority of Christ is involved in them, and we
must either be prepared to let that faith go as a
thing of no value, or we must be prepared to
adopt the ground which many seem disposed to
suggest; which is not " I believe what I believe
because it is *true* and I believe it to be *true*,"
but "I believe certain things though I see there
is ground to believe they, or many of them, are
not true, and I intend to continue to believe them
because in many ways it is expedient to do so,
even though they be not true, or there is ground
for questioning whether they are so. In short,
I hold my faith in solution, and am content
to do so." Critics and philosophers may be left
to decide whether this is critical or philosoph-
ical. I believe it to be absolutely opposed to

the mind and teaching of the New Testament, and I am determined to seek some better basis for my faith than that which destructive criticism can supply.

For example, it is impossible for a man to say that he accepts the Apostles' Creed, and theoretically to disbelieve in the supernatural. Neither do I see how it is possible for a man to acknowledge the literal meaning of the word "Christ," and reject that basis of Divine prophecy, promise, and action in the Old Testament without which that word has no real significance. Some minds take delight in dissolving and analyzing these elements. I confess that I prefer to rest on the substantial constructive basis that they present, and which, as it seems to me, they inevitably indicate and point to, dissolve and analyze them as we may.

It is symptomatic of much of the thought of the present day that those miraculous elements in the Gospels, for instance, which at the time were doubtless given and received as confirmatory of its message, are now regarded as the main obstacle in its reception. There must surely be something wrong here. In the first place we may well question how far the gospel can be received apart from its miraculous setting, or what sort of a gospel that is that remains after the miraculous has been rejected; and secondly, this important fact remains, that the belief in the miraculous is not proposed as an end in itself, but is intended to point and lead up to something which is higher and beyond the miracle itself, and which, if it is not grasped, the miracle itself is worthless; and there can be no doubt that if this end is apprehended, the miracle may be largely left to take care of itself. It is more to believe in Christ than it is to believe that He turned water into wine or fed five thousand with a few loaves and fishes; but it is equally hard to determine what kind of faith in Christ that would be, or whether it could rightly be called faith at all, which professed to believe in Him and yet stumbled at the feeding of the five thousand or the miracle of Cana in Galilee. If one believes in Christ one believes in His mighty works. He himself contemplates belief in His mighty works without belief in Him. I hardly think it can be said that He contemplates a belief in Him which would reject His mighty works. "Believe me that I am in the Father and the Father in me; or else believe *me* for the very works' sake."

And this, as it seems to me, is the true position with regard to the miraculous. It is involved in sincere belief in Christ, and though that belief may not be *based* on the miraculous, it can scarcely be said to be independent of it. If we ask whether the miracles prove the Gospel or the Gospel proves the miracles we may decide in favor of both; and certainly if the Gospel proves the miracles, as it surely does, we cannot refuse to admit that the miracles confirm the Gospel. They are mutually dependent, though the order of them may be doubtful in point of evidence.

It may seem that I have, to a certain extent, wandered from the question I proposed to consider, in thus mixing up the Old and New Testaments in the discussion; but, in point of fact, the ground is common to both. There is an indestructible connection between the Old Testament and the New, which it is impossible to disregard. And if one treats the Old Testament in such a way as to make it inadequate as a prime factor in the production of the New, we do more than damage and depreciate the Old Testament; because we stultify ourselves, inasmuch as we have left unaccounted-for a series of literary and historical facts as an effect which we have deprived of its only sufficient and pos-

sible cause. For it is absolutely certain that
if the documents of the Old Testament actually
were of the character that the extreme criticism
assigns to them, they would have been impotent
to produce either the literature of the New Testament or the historic facts which it relates and
to which it testifies. Suppose, for example, that
we regard the whole book of Psalms as a product
of the second century before Christ, to what in-
extricable confusion do we not only reduce the
entire volume of the Old Testament, but how
preposterously ignorant must we presume both
Christ and His enemies to have been, who were
evidently most grossly mistaken as to their true
history and origin. In fact, it would not be difficult to show that the way the Old Testament is
referred to, and the use that is made of it in the
New, is incontrovertible proof that the various
documents were no modern production, but must
have required ages to build up and consolidate
in the form they had then assumed. Anything,
therefore, which ignores and disregards this fact,
is on that very ground self-condemned. There
are certain characteristics about the work of
time which it is impossible to counterfeit, and
it is contrary to all precedent that documents
in the second century of their existence should

have acquired the reputation for an antiquity of ten or twelve. And here is one of those broad features of evidence which the layman and the man in the street are as capable of appreciating and apprehending as the most profound scholar, and probably more so.

As long, then, as the ordinary reader is possessed of his Bible in the vernacular, he will be as capable of estimating not only its substantive message, but certain broad features also of its form and fabric as the expert and the scholar; and so far as he is proof against theories which are the offspring only of hypotheses, and unbiased by them, it is quite possible that he may form a sounder, more correct judgment than the critic who, enamoured of his own theories, and blinded by their apparent symmetry and supposed exigencies, is, in order to save his own credit, compelled to shut his eyes to facts that may nevertheless be too solid and substantial to be overthrown.

LECTURE II

In my former lecture I endeavored to form some idea of what the Old Testament really is, and what its claims are upon our attention. I showed that it was impossible so to exhaust the Old Testament of the supernatural as to leave in it sufficient vitality and motive power to be either explicable in itself, or to serve as the immediate parent and progenitor of the facts and literature of the New Testament. For though it is very evident that the supernatural facts of the Old Testament are frequently alluded to in the literature, yet that literature has evidently not been produced merely by the facts, but by the belief in an almighty competent and favoring Power to whom the facts bore witness. It was not the thunders of Sinai which impressed themselves permanently on the minds of the people, but the personal being and presence of that God to whom they bore such tremendous testimony. And so the possession of Canaan, full as the history of it was with the miraculous, served not so much to recall those wonders as to witness to the promises to the fathers of which it was the abiding proof.

Thus even in the Old Testament, if rightly understood, it is not the supernatural which is the pre-
eminent and obtrusive feature, but the power and
presence, the majesty and holiness, of that God
who made use of these features to awaken in
men's minds the conception and consciousness of
His presence. When and where this was done,
the function of the miraculous might cease, and
the need for it pass away; but it would by no
means follow that it had never been employed, or
had never been wanted.

I shall now draw attention to certain other
characteristics of the Old Testament which seem
to me to be almost as eloquent as the miraculous
itself in favor of the divine character and claims
of the Old Testament, and try to determine how
far they are affected by critical theories concerning
the various books. First, there is the oft repeated
promise to Abraham, for which there seems no
natural motive at any period, or in any event of
the history; that is to say, not the promise of the
land, which is intelligible, but the promise of
blessing for all nations, which was in strong contrast to the national exclusiveness. No theory of
the higher criticism suffices to explain this, still
less the fact that ages afterwards it became a
germinal principle of immense vitality.

Then take the promise to Moses : "If ye will
obey my voice indeed and keep my covenant,
then ye shall be a peculiar treasure unto me
above all the peoples; for all the earth is mine,
and ye shall be unto me a kingdom of priests and
a holy nation." This has been put on a level
with the claim of other nations to the protection
and favor of their deities ; but surely the difference is patent. In every other nation it is the
deity whom the nation chooses and worships, and
the protection of the deity is regarded as more or
less a thing which the deity is pledged to be-
stow ; but the conception of a kingdom of priests
and a holy nation finds no parallel elsewhere, any
more than the Scriptural idea of holiness itself
does. Here, again, we may point to a principle
which did not manifest the fulness of its inherent vitality till ages afterwards. Nor can we discover any period in the national history when
this sentiment is likely to have suggested itself
to any known historian ; but here we find it communicated to Moses in the secret visions of the
mount. I submit that it is not the form or circumstances of the narrative that require to be
accounted for or elucidated, but the substance of
the communication itself, which indeed is explicable only on the supposition of its truth. The

higher criticism gives us no explanation of this, but only offers some trivial conjecture as to the composition of the narrative. It is the same with all the more striking and graphic incidents of the history of the exodus and the wanderings, such as the breaking of the tables of stone and the prayer of Moses thereupon; the promise " my presence shall go with thee and I will give thee rest;" the proclamation of the name of the Lord as merciful and gracious, which is continually manifesting its influence in the subsequent literature; the prescribed form of blessing for the children of Israel, with its mysterious triple articulation; the promise often repeated afterwards, "as truly as I live all the earth shall be filled with the glory of the Lord;" the forty years' wanderings in consequence of rebellion and murmuring; the marvellous history and the thwarted endeavors of Balaam to curse the people. These and a hundred other things are among the indelible features of the Mosaic narrative; and I repeat that the higher criticism offers not one fragment of explanation to account for or explain them as they are, but only theorizes in a paltry and childish way about their particular form and the profound problem to which of the letters of the alphabet they are severally to be referred. But surely even

in a fictitious narrative it is the essential substance rather than the accidents of form that
demand our primary attention and regard, and the
question of questions in relation to these various
incidents is their inherent truth or falsehood. If
they are fictions then the form and incidents of
their composition are matters of the utmost triv-
iality ; but if there is in them the substance and
soul of truth, they then become matters of the
highest import, and the special feature of their form
may be left to take care of itself as a thing of
very small importance. The tendency which this
kind of treatment betrays has very much the ap-
pearance of a covert attack upon the veritable
truth of the narrative under the pretence of a
minute examination of its form, which is after all
purely subjective and can lead to no tangible or
valid result.

When we come to the Book of Deuteronomy
the issue presented is very definite and unmistakable. For either from first to last the assumed narrative is a fiction designed to represent
the imaginary action of Moses, or it is what it
manifestly pretends to be, the personal narrative
of the last days of the lawgiver. If it really is this,
its value is unquestionably incalculable ; if it is
not, it is equally impossible to determine what

its value is ; but one thing is absolutely certain, that historically its value is *nil*. And yet there are sentiments and incidents in this book of the highest possible literary value ; but if their historic reality is taken from them, it is not only difficult to gauge their true value, but also hard to conceive how as mere inventions they can have entered into the head of any man, and how, at the time supposed, they should have been so concocted by an unknown writer as to deceive alike the king, the high priest, and the prophetess, who one and all accepted them as the personal narrative of Moses some seven centuries before.

Not only is truth stranger than fiction, but in certain cases fiction seems to gather itself together to be more extravagant than truth, and for very spite to outbid and to defy truth. And this case of the production of Deuteronomy under the conditions supposed would seem to be one of them. Deuteronomy is precisely one of those compositions of which on purely *à priori* and subjective principles it is difficult to determine the character. Did we know nothing of its history we might hesitate to say whether it was truth or fiction. But can any one venture to say that we know nothing of its history ? It comes before us with a continuous pedigree of three thousand years on the one side; and on the other there is nothing but conjecture. Surely the presumption is enormously in favor of its truth, and beyond all doubt the *onus probandi* rests and must rest on the attempt to prove it fiction. There is no need to bias the issue by the use of the word "forgery." The question simply is whether Deuteronomy is a true or fictitious narrative. And this on purely abstract principles it may be difficult, or even, for lack of data, impossible to decide. But is there, strictly speaking, here any lack of data? Undoubtedly not, unless we summarily reject the data that do exist. But that surely is a most unwarrantable proceeding when there is nothing but conjecture on the other side. It is beyond all doubt that, as far as literary evidence goes, there is continuous and unbroken testimony alike to the existence and to the influence of Deuteronomy; and unless we are to assume that all this complex and apparently undesigned evidence has been intentionally and fraudulently fabricated and arranged for the purpose of producing the effect as we perceive it, the criteria in favor of Deuteronomy must be presumed complete and conclusive. Except on the assumption of the most gigantic and systematic

imposture, or the most obstinate and elaborate
self-deception, it is impossible to set aside the
testimony of Deuteronomy. And if in this case
it is set aside, it is hard to know what literary
production can be regarded as secure. For there
is perhaps scarcely any one literary production
of antiquity so well attested as Deuteronomy. If
Deuteronomy, therefore, is not genuine, it is hard
to determine what literary production may not
be called in question. Deuteronomy, moreover,
furnishes an excellent test of the principle that
the ethical value of a narrative does not depend
on its historical truth. For surely no one could
maintain that the ethical value of Deuteronomy
would be the same whether it were fiction or a
narrative of fact. If the relation between the
Creator and the lawgiver were such as is repre-
sented in Deuteronomy, it stands to reason that
the ethical value of the narrative must be far
greater than if the narrative were a fiction. And
yet if the narrative was put together seven
hundred years after the time of Moses, it is
equally certain that it can have no value as
history, if only for the reason that it is alleged
to be at variance with the history in Exodus
and Numbers. So far, then, as this is the case
and if it be so, we must decide which is true,

and shall probably come to the conclusion that
neither is.[1]

In like manner when we pass to the historical
books, we surely must decide whether they are
to be received as history or regarded as myth.
Are they *bonâ fide*, or written with a bias? and if
the bias can be detected, is it of such a nature
as to vitiate the substance of the narrative? It
may be said that these are all questions independent of the higher criticism, with which it
does not concern itself; and so they may be, but
there is an antecedent question, to which I am
determined to find an answer; and that is, What
is the substantive value of these historical documents? — before we begin to subject them to
vivisection; and possibly it may turn out that
they would be altogether undeserving of this
microscopic attention, were it not that they are
legitimately entitled to the claim which is denied them. If they really are the tissue of
misrepresentation and deception they are alleged
to be, surely they would not be worthy of the
pains bestowed upon them. It is because of
their inherited claim, and practically for this
alone, that they are so vehemently attacked.
And yet there is so much of the stamp of the

---

[1] Driver's Deuteronomy, p. xxxv *et seq.*

supernatural upon them as might suffice to give us pause before rejecting them out of hand. For take the books of Samuel and Kings in their broadest and most every-day aspect, do they not record the longing of the nation for a king, the unsuccessful issue of the first attempt, the choice of an insignificant person to be the anointed king to whom the perpetual possession of the throne was promised? And is it not a fact that after this man's line had been set aside, and the monarchy cleft in two, the rival line turned out to be little better than a succession of usurpers, while the lineal descendant of the chosen king was still in possession of his fathers' throne, when four hundred years afterwards the nation and monarchy were finally dissolved and broken up? I do not see how at any period after Solomon the fiction of perpetuity in David's line is likely to have been attributed to him or his time if it was really a later invention, because in that case there was so much to contradict it in notorious facts; and yet as an undoubted truth the last King of Judah was the lineal descendant of David. Now, I do not know that there is any point in this chain of circumstances that is open to dispute, unless it be the original promise to David, which, if a fact, ad-

mits of no natural explanation; and yet it is
this very promise to which, as we have seen, it
is so difficult to assign a late origin. Nor do I
know of any way in which it can be dealt with
other than that of Ewald and Dean Stanley, who
deliberately disregarded it and chose to represent
the line of Israel as the legitimate and natural
line in which the monarchy was perpetuated, in
manifest defiance, however, of all the facts.

But then how full are these books themselves
of graphic and life-like portraits and incidents
which must forever entitle them to a unique
and unrivalled position in the historical literature of the world. Take the characters of Samuel, Saul, David, Elijah, Elisha, Ahab, Jehu, and
the rest, and the various incidents connected
with them, and are there not stamped upon
them the indelible features of a God-given history? And if the footprints of God are to be
traced anywhere in human history, is it not
here, in a history claiming to be guided by
Him, that we may trace them most plainly
and unmistakably?

Then, again, take the Psalms, which occupy an
absolutely unique position in the literature of the
world; to which there is no true analogy, and
most undoubtedly no rival. The question may

well be asked, What has the higher criticism done
for the Psalms? And the answer is, To refer them
all to the second century before Christ. But with
what result? And the answer is, To make them
absolutely unintelligible, inconsistent, and impossible. What elucidation does the 110th Psalm,
so clearly referred to in Zech. vi. 13, in the sixth
century B. C., and with which Zechariah was manifestly familiar, gain by being thus assigned to
the second century? Whatever light it had
before becomes gross darkness; and if the witness of language is of any weight at all, how
are we to account for its archaic character here?
and what possible connection has the allusion to
Melchisedec here? Take, again, the 51st Psalm,
which all tradition has associated with David's
repentance; does it become more intelligible or
more appropriate by being assigned to a writer
and occasion utterly unknown, and seven or eight
centuries later? Instead of elucidating the literature, criticism of this kind effectually obscures
and darkens it. On the other hand, accepting
the 51st Psalm as David's, the words " Purge me
with hyssop and I shall be clean" furnish undesigned but conclusive evidence of the writer's
acquaintance with the Levitical ordinances, inasmuch as hyssop is mentioned only here, and

4

once in relation to the physical knowledge of Solomon, besides its sevenfold mention in connection with those ordinances. I am at a loss to know what is gained by affirming, contrary to all testimony, and without the slightest positive ground, that the superscription to the 51st Psalm is not genuine, confirmed as it is by the Septuagint and Syriac; whereas if we trust it, as we surely may, the Psalm at once receives an accession of illumination from the known history of the writer. Is it not a fact that our own hymnology is heightened in interest and significance when we can associate the several hymns with the personal recollections of Toplady, Cowper, or Lyte? Should we gain or lose by being told by some critic of the twentieth century that " Rock of Ages cleft for me," had been wrongly ascribed to its traditional author, and was an unknown composition of an unknown date; or that " God moves in a mysterious way," was not written by Cowper; or " Abide with Me," by Lyte? The unlearned public is disposed to attach an undue importance to the assertions of those who arrogate to themselves the appellation of critics, which in a large number of cases have about as much ground to rest on as the instances now suggested would have. In nearly all cases subjective hy-

pothesis usurps the place of objective evidence;
and every one knows that the same object as-
sumes an entirely different aspect according to
the position of the person regarding it.

Take, again, the 80th Psalm, which is ascribed
to Asaph. The second verse of that Psalm is
absolutely unintelligible unless it refers to an obscure passage in the so-called Priestly Code of the
Pentateuch. The appeal is, "Before Ephraim and
Benjamin and Manasseh stir up thy strength, and
come and save us," — those being the very tribes
which followed the ark during the march in the
desert. Now, this Psalm is ascribed to Asaph,
the contemporary of David, and the Priestly
Code is assigned to the fifth century before
Christ. Consequently, we must infer that Asaph
was acquainted with the order of march in the
wilderness, which, as there is no other record of
it, he must have learned from the Priestly Code,
which therefore must have existed in his time; or,
accepting the hypothetical date of the critics for
that supposititious document, we must infer that
a still later writer seized upon this casual statement of the newly invented code, and made it
the basis of his appeal to the Shepherd of Israel
at a time when Ephraim, Benjamin, and Manasseh had all been dispersed in captivity and had

no longer any independent tribal existence. Is this in the remotest degree probable? But unless it is, the other inference, which points to a time before the division of the monarchy, and to the knowledge at that time of the order of the march in the desert, must be allowed its full weight; and, accepting the authorship of the Psalm, it must rank as evidence of the existence of the Pentateuch in the time of David. Two incidental references such as these in the 51st and 80th Psalms, it must be confessed, carry us not a little way towards a decision as to the date of the records of the Pentateuch.

The book of Psalms, moreover, is a treasury of devotion of the broadest possible character; for it is the fullest and freest expression of the personal relation of the soul to God. In this respect it is unrivalled and invaluable. And its association with some of the well-known servants of God must be held to add enormously to its authority and value; but if we put aside all the inscriptions, and refer its authorship to obscure and unknown writers of the second century B. C., and that upon simply baseless hypothetical considerations, we may indeed have achieved a triumph of criticism, but we have no less certainly succeeded in depreciating and rendering worthless the value of the Psalms as an authorized treasury of devotion. Indeed, this is the very point, it seems to me, that we have to determine: How far is the Book of Psalms an authorized treasury of devotion, and on what does that authority depend? Is the authority of the Book of Psalms something it derives from its place in the canon, or is its place in the canon merely a witness to its authority? and if so, from what is that authority derived? Now, the authority of the Psalms is to a large extent dependent upon the truth and reality of the statements therein contained. For example: "The Lord hath said unto me, Thou art my son; this day have I begotten thee." "I will instruct thee, and teach thee in the way which thou shalt go: I will guide thee with mine eye." "Hear, O my people, and I will speak; O Israel, and I will testify against thee; I am God, even thy God." "Call upon me in the time of trouble: I will deliver thee, and thou shalt glorify me." "God hath spoken in his holiness; I will rejoice, I will divide Shechem, and mete out the valley of Succoth." These and a hundred other statements throw us back upon the question, Have they merely subjective assurance, or do they rest upon objective certainty? If they are merely the sub-

jective assertion of confidence, then they are more
or less untrue and unauthorized in their assertion ; but if they are true, then their truth is not
one that we must look for in the heart of the
writer, but one that rests on the objective declaration of the professed speaker ; that is, on the
actual revelation and promise of God. This of
course presupposes the fact of revelation, but it
is a very serious question whether it is possible
to account for the confident language of the
Psalms except on the supposition of a positive
revelation of God. If all the statements in the
Psalms are resolved into subjective expressions
of assurance, then there is an end to everything
like authority unless it can be shown that they
are otherwise authoritative ; and how is this to
be shown apart from the objective facts upon
which they are supposed to rest ? Either it is a
fact that God spoke to David, or it is not. If it is
not, then all the assertions in the Psalms to that
effect are false and delusive. If it is, then these
assertions are the proof of it ; but in that case
there is a reality for them to rest on, and we have
something to which we can appeal as the veritable
word of God ; and the place of the Psalms in the
canon is a witness to this word of God, but by no
means the cause of its being the word of God.

And this, I take it, is a very significant difference which the higher criticism does not face and
cannot explain, but can only try to explain away,
to the absolute destruction of anything like faith.
The Psalms, therefore, must be regarded as a
storehouse of unwarrantable assurance, having
no foundation in itself, and supplying none to
any one else ; or, on the contrary, they are the
expression of hopes and confidences which were
breathed into the hearts of the writers by the
spirit of the living God, and which for that reason have the power for all time of awakening the
like confidence and assurance in every one who
will trust in like manner in the same living and
eternal God, who is ever ready to establish and
confirm His word.

Another function, however, which the Psalms
fulfil is in the testimony that they give to the
main facts of the national history ; and this is
independent and spontaneous testimony that it
is not possible to rebut. We have the history of
the exodus and the wanderings, the wonders of
the conquest and the struggle of the Judges,
no less than the promise to David and the fortunes of the tabernacle, borne witness to in the
national poetry of the Psalms. So that they are
to the history of Israel what the historical plays

of Shakespeare are to that of England. That
is to say, they presuppose a framework of events,
and that in this case of a supernatural character,
apart from which they could have had no existence; and though in each case it may be possible
to minimize the supernatural element, it is not
possible to deny that the net result is such as
to leave, as it is clearly intended to leave, no doubt
in the reader's mind that God dealt with Israel
as He did not deal with any other nation. The
national history is the unmistakable witness to
this fact, and the national poetry confirms it.

There are three institutions characteristic of
Israel which are highly significant and important,
the rare mention of which in certain parts of the
Old Testament may help us to estimate the value
of the argument from silence so often appealed
to: these are, the tabernacle, the Sabbath, and
circumcision. It is one of the achievements of
the higher criticism to have demolished the tabernacle and to have proved, or rather shown
(which, be it remembered, is not the same thing),
that it never had any existence whatever except
on paper and in the imagination of Babylonian
priests. But, of course, this can only be done by
setting aside not only the prescriptions of the
Pentateuch, but also by disregarding the evidence

of the books of Joshua and Samuel, to say nothing of the testimony of the 78th Psalm, "So that he forsook the tabernacle of Shiloh, the tent, which he placed among men," confirmed as this is by the prophet Jeremiah, vii. 12, 14, and xxvi. 9. Surely it is not all at once that the people of England or of this country are likely to be persuaded to accept a theory so monstrous in the face of direct and positive evidence to the contrary, merely because a few German critics have suggested the notion, and a few English scholars have adopted it to the infinite discredit of their own judgment. Does it not seem to surpass the limits of possibility that a body of exiled priests in Babylon should amuse themselves with sketching out in minute and laborious detail the plan and measurements of an imaginary tabernacle created only by their own conception. The very idea seems to court rejection; and yet, strange to say, there are those to whom it seems more probable than that the pattern shown to Moses in the mount should be preserved in Exodus.

Again, with regard to the Sabbath, often as it is mentioned in the last four books of the Pentateuch, the word does not occur in Genesis, though there are slight indications of acquaintance with the institution; but it is not so much

as named in any historical book before 2 Kings,
and only once in the title of one of the Psalms.
Five only of the fifteen prophets make any allusion to it; so that were it not for its constant
occurrence in the Pentateuch and the later historical books, one might almost question the
knowledge, or at least the observance of it.

Still more remarkable is the case of circumcision. The original charter of it is given in
Genesis xvii., which is assigned by the critics
to the fifth century B. C.; after the Book of
Joshua, there is but one solitary allusion to circumcision in Jeremiah (ix. 25), and yet I suppose
no one would question the fact that this rite was
practised by the Israelites from the very first;
and the fact that the Arabs still practise it in
the thirteenth year, that being the age at which
Ishmael was circumcised, is a strong confirmation thereof. But how is all this consistent
with the theory that the 17th chapter of Genesis was written in the fifth century B. C., and
that, without any written precept, the nation
had universally practised it for fifteen centuries before? Is this conceivable? Is it possible?
Are not the practical difficulties involved in
the theory far greater than they would be on
the supposition that the original command was

given to Abraham as recorded in Genesis? If otherwise, what evidence is there that circumcision had any ground to be regarded as the veritable sign of God's covenant?

To take the parallel case of baptism. Suppose that it could be shown that all our Lord's commands respecting baptism were thirteen centuries later than his time; how would it be possible to maintain that baptism was anything more than an ecclesiastical rite resting upon no divine authority and proving no divine sanction? And yet this is what would inevitably follow in the case of Israel with regard to circumcision, if it were admitted that Genesis xvii. were of the fifth century B. C. In short, the one question we have to settle is, What constitutes the authority of the Old Testament, and who gave it that authority? Now, to put it broadly, if Moses is the ultimate author of the Pentateuch, then the authority of the Pentateuch is the authority of Moses. He was the mediator of the covenant therein contained. It was by and through him that God dealt with Israel after the manner therein narrated. But I fail to see where this authority is to come from, or how it is to be communicated to a series of documents written by nobody knows who, and not committed to writing till seven hundred or eight hundred years afterwards, it being at the same time affirmed that Moses was to a large extent a mythical personage, and that the greatest uncertainty hangs over all his history. This surely would be to postulate a theory of revelation without any credentials, and to accept it merely because it had been traditionally regarded as a revelation, though the reasons when investigated were by no means apparent. And yet this is the alternative to which we are committed if we reject the substantial historic truth of the Mosaic narrative. If it is not of Moses, to whom can we ascribe it whose name would carry with it one tithe of the like authority? Nay, how could we be sure that it would possess any authority at all? I suppose that it is admitted generally that any document to be authoritative must be able to furnish credentials which shall authenticate it. If Deuteronomy was written in the age of Manasseh or Josiah, what are its credentials? They are manifestly *nil*, except so far as its adoption by the king, high priest, prophetess, and people supplied them, — credentials which, however, *they* were unable to supply if they did not exist. In like manner, if Moses is the ultimate author of the Exodus narrative, its credentials are supplied by that fact; if it was seven hundred or eight hundred years later it can possess no credentials at all, and can "only in a bare nucleus be Mosaic;" that is, must be more mythical than true. What I want to know is, whether this is the way in which we are prepared to accept the Old Testament narrative at the bidding of self-styled critics; because in that case we must entirely remodify all our traditional belief, even as that is adopted and expressed in the New Testament.

I come now to the Prophets, about which criticism has been unusually busy with regard to date. In the Hebrew canon there are fifteen prophets, — three greater and twelve lesser prophets. With regard to the general date of Isaiah, Jeremiah, and Ezekiel there is no reasonable doubt. With regard to the minor prophets, their arrangement in the Hebrew canon is manifestly that of ante and post-captivity prophets; and in the former case, the division is into those of the Assyrian and Babylonian periods. The general correctness of this arrangement is admitted, but with regard to one of the earlier prophets, namely Joel, it has been rashly conjectured that he belonged to the post-captivity period. Now, as the canonical arrangement is

undoubtedly in the main correct, it seems haz-
ardous to interfere with it in the case of Joel,
unless it is absolutely necessary to do so. But
the main reason advanced is because the evidence borne by Joel to the early acquaintance
with the Levitical ritual is so strong as to be
absolutely fatal to the supposed late origin of the
law. This, however, is setting aside evidence
rather than being guided by it, and consequently
Joel may be allowed to retain his place until
stronger reasons can be given for removing him
from it.

The book of the prophet Isaiah, however, has
been the battlefield of controversy; though in this
case also the positive and external testimony is
distinctly in favor of its integrity, and is only to
be rebutted by subjective interpretation of internal phenomena. We have this fact to deal
with, that at the time of Christ all the writings
ascribed to Isaiah were acknowledged and quoted
as his; there is no vestige of any other belief.
Therefore the guardians of the canon must have
been guilty of extreme and culpable carelessness
if they joined on to the writings of Isaiah the work
of an unknown man who lived a century and a
half later, and preserved no record of his work or
personality. This on the face of it appears to be

highly improbable; and, moreover, several chapters are expressly assigned to Isaiah, as the 2d, 13th, etc. Of these, the 13th could never have been so assigned but on the belief that there was nothing inherently improbable in its being his, whereas it is precisely on this ground that it is now denied to him. The conception, therefore, of the function of the prophet in the two cases differs, and the one is inconsistent with the other; but it is this inconsistency which is the basis of the criticism. Those who were responsible for the canon assumed that the prophet could have written every chapter in the book; it is because the critics assume that he could not that they reject his authorship. The prophet, we are told, speaks from the standpoint of his own time. That may be so, but the horizon of his vision extends far beyond his own time. A prophet who could have written the first or sixth chapters of Isaiah was certainly not limited by the horizon of his own time, and if there is no foreknowledge in either it is hard to say where it may be found, in the last twenty-seven chapters or elsewhere. For assuredly it is not only in the writings of the prophets that we may discover it, but many times over in every book of the Pentateuch, as well as in the other historical books. In short,

it is this feature of anticipation and foreknowledge which stamps the Old Testament as a
whole, and it is impossible to get rid of it by
assigning a later date to this or that passage
ascribed to an earlier prophet. For example,
even allowing that the standpoint of the last
twenty-seven chapters is that of the captivity,
which, however, I by no means allow, this in no
degree accounts for their most characteristic phenomena. The fact that Cyrus is twice mentioned
by name, and Babylon and the Chaldeans some
four or five times in these chapters, by no means
proves that that is their chief subject-matter.
On the contrary, there is a vast amount of
matter with which they have nothing whatever
to do, and which is equally inexplicable whether
it is referred to the sixth or to the eighth century
before Christ. And so with the notorious 53d
chapter. Let it be assigned to any one person on whom the critics can agree, so that it
be not Jesus Christ, it nevertheless remains, and
will remain a fact to all time, that there is no
conceivable character in all history to whom it
has so close an apparent reference, no one whom
it so vividly portrays, and no one to whom it so
naturally belongs, as to the suffering Saviour.
Whether the writer lived five hundred or seven

hundred years before Christ it matters not; for history presents us with no conceivable subject for his canvas; and if he unconsciously produced an ideal portrait of Christ, that is an achievement as far beyond the natural powers of a post-captivity writer as it was beyond the natural powers of Isaiah, and therefore exegesis gains nothing by putting this composition a century and a half or two centuries later than the prophet's time. Anyhow we are confronted with a phenomenon for which there is no natural or sufficient explanation, and every attempt to explain it sinks into nothing before that which was given by Philip the Evangelist to the Ethiopian eunuch. And on the supposition that that is in any sense intentional and correct, it defies all ingenuity to account for its existence or its creation at any period between the time of Isaiah and the closing of the canon. The critics, therefore, are only throwing dust in our eyes when they think to persuade us that they can eviscerate the superhuman and divine elements inherent in the Old Testament, or can reduce it to the level of a merely human production by shifting the date of some of its documents, and interpreting its utterances of the barren and the commonplace. " If not a line of Hebrew prophecy had been written

till after the captivity of the Jews in Babylon,
there is a mass of matter remaining which must
have been as purely predictive in substance as it
is in form." [1]

It is here, in the interests of truth and faith,
that criticism compels us to take our stand, because it is on the Divine authority and the Divine
character of these books that we depend; and if
this is destroyed the ground is taken away from
under our feet, for the Old Testament is worth
nothing if it can be proved to be only from man,
and of the earth earthy. And therefore it is impossible for us, as believing men, to regard with
equanimity conclusions and hypotheses which,
though baseless, nevertheless assume trium-
phantly that their position is established, and
their results unassailable; for if this be so,
most unquestionably faith is made void, and the
promises made of none effect.

The last nine chapters of Ezekiel are unique
not only among the writings of the prophets,
but also among the books of the Bible. They
present a strong contrast to the rest of his own
book, for they give an ideal picture of the restored
polity and ritual of the emancipated nation;
and yet there is no evidence of their ever having

---

[1] Duke of Argyll, " Philosophy of Belief," p. 267.

had the slightest influence on the conduct and history of the returning captives. Nor is it even possible that they can have been written with that intent; for many of the features and conditions supposed are physically impossible and can never have been meant to be realized. On the supposition, however, that what is called the Priestly Code was the product of the priests of the exile, it is the more remarkable that it should have varied so widely from the prophetic ideal. For here, it may be presumed, was a precedent of high authority in existence, put forth by a recognized prophet in the most solemn manner; and yet, without any reference to this, the unknown and unauthorized priests of the exile are supposed to have sketched out precepts and have prescribed rites of their own, which they had the audacity to represent as given by God to Moses a thousand years before. Is it at all within the limits of possibility that the returning exiles should have at once hailed these fabrications as the prescriptions of Moses and have consented to adopt them? Is there any parallel case within the annals of history? I greatly doubt it, and am persuaded that the thing in itself is impossible; and yet this is the theory which is advanced for the purpose of displacing the traditional authenticity and antiquity of the Mosaic law.

There is another feature with regard to the prophet Ezekiel which does not seem to have been fully recognized. It is forgotten that he was one of the captives and passed his life in captivity, and yet on several occasions he speaks of and describes events in the home of his fathers as though he were present in Jerusalem. So that the spirit of prophecy, it would seem, revealed to him things distant in space of which otherwise he could have had no knowledge. We must determine whether or not this was so, as it certainly seems to have been; but if it was, it presents a remarkable analogy to the more common function of prophecy, which is to depict things distant in time. Now as prediction pure and simple is denied to be one of the functions of prophecy, we may also ask whether the vision of things distant in space is likewise beyond the power of the spirit of God, and whether the evidence of its not being so, in Ezekiel for example, is also to be set aside; for if not, there would seem to be no reason for denying the analogous power of depicting things distant in time as a legitimate function of prophecy.

There is one other book of the Old Testament which demands independent notice, and that is the book of Daniel, which from the times of Porphyry

onwards has been the favorite butt of unbeliev-
ing criticism. Now, here it must be borne in
mind that the book of Daniel is beset with difficulties, in consequence mainly of our own lack of
knowledge. For example, the identification of
Darius the Mede and the history of Belshazzar
present questions that are not capable of final
solution. But it is so often forgotten that the
impossibility of obtaining absolute certainty is no
reason for rejecting the balance of probability.
If probability is the guide of life we ought not to
reject its indications when certain knowledge is
unattainable. Now let us suppose that Daniel is
the romance of an unknown writer in the second
century. It is admitted on all hands that he had
a very considerable minute knowledge of the
times and manners which he depicts. That he may
have made some mistakes is of course possible.
But how much probability is there in his going
out of the way, as he clearly has, to perpetrate
such a blunder as to speak of Darius the Mede
and to mention his age? It is hardly conceivable
that he did not know how grossly he was expos-
ing himself to the charge of ignorance and in-
accuracy; and this is certainly some reason for
crediting him with the possession of knowledge
that we lack ourselves. To confound Darius the

Mede with Darius Hystaspes, in the second century before Christ, is surely more improbable than that the true Daniel three centuries and a half before should have possessed knowledge that has passed away. The very fact of a presumed blot like this on a document in many other respects exact, may be taken with more probability as evidence of special acquaintance than as betokening unpardonable ignorance and error.

Then, with regard to the supposed Greek words in Daniel, I take it we know too little of the conditions of intercourse between Greece and Babylonia in the sixth century before Christ to pronounce with certainty on a definite point of detail like this. It is known, however, that Antimenidas, a brother of the poet Alcæus, served as a soldier in the army of Nebuchadnezzar. Now, one fact of this kind is sufficient to outweigh much conjectural hypothesis based on philological inference. If Daniel is genuine, then the use of these words speaks for itself. On the other hand, any inference drawn from their occurrence is hardly sufficient to disprove its genuineness, though it readily serves as one item in the indictment to the contrary.

The question of the genuineness of Daniel, however, is too large to be discussed here; but

one or two considerations of weight may be
thrown out by the way. For instance, we learn
from Ezekiel that Daniel was a well-known personage of the captivity; that he had a reputation
for righteousness and wisdom; and this is all that
we know. Is it at all likely that three centuries
and a half afterwards a romance should have
been made out of these slender materials by an
unknown writer, and should have been developed
into our existing book of Daniel? For in addition
to this, there is no question but that the romance
so concocted rapidly made its way as an authentic
history, as we see from the allusion to it in the
first book of Maccabees, and the position assigned
to it in the Gospels.

In short, it seems to me that the balance of
probability is largely on the side of the genuineness of Daniel; though here, as elsewhere, absolute certainty may be unattainable, or rather it
is impossible to foreclose every avenue of doubt;
and, what must never be forgotten, its genuineness and authenticity are so heavily weighted
with the miraculous and the incredible. After
all, the prophecy of the fifth empire, which fore-
shadows the kingdom of heaven, and that of the
seventy weeks, which will fit into the death of
Christ as it will fit into nothing else, are vir-

tual challenges in favor of its genuineness; for neither prophecy was more within the range of the vision of an unknown and unauthorized writer in the second century B. C. than it was within that of the "man greatly beloved," who declared himself so highly favored with the visions of God. Here, as elsewhere, the substantive truth of the narrative has a direct bearing upon its genuineness; for, if it is not genuine, then it is impossible to regard the personal details otherwise recorded than as audacious falsehoods simply thrown into the narrative as garniture, and to commend the book as ministering to an unhealthy appetite for the marvellous.

On the other hand, it seems to me impossible to read the book of Daniel and not feel that there is that in it which is more incongruous with its supposed fiction than the wonders related, however explained, would be under the circumstances as recorded, with its truth. If Daniel really was the "man greatly beloved," the chosen and honored representative of his nation at the court of his captors, it does not seem out of harmony with the recorded action of God in other ages, if we believe the record, that his career should be specially marked by special interposition. Here, again, we are thrown back upon the old question of miracles and a supernatural revelation. We are reminded over and over again that "miracles do not happen." For my own part I very strongly demur to *this* statement; but if we once accept it, then the next question must surely be, "Did they ever happen?" And so far as this springs out of the other *dictum*, it may, nay, *must*, in like manner be decided; but of this it would seem we may be absolutely certain: that it is equally impossible to read the Old Testament or the New and not find ourselves confronted with miracle, which we must either put aside at once, as of no account, or accept; but which, whatever its relation to the substance of the record, it is wholly impossible to account for, and which therefore must either be taken as intended, in the providence of God, to confirm the narrative and commend its acceptance, or must be regarded as vitiating and discrediting the narrative, and as for that reason to be rejected together with the narrative so discredited.

www.ingramcontent.com/pod-product-compliance
Lightning Source LLC
Chambersburg PA
CBHW020237090426
42735CB00010B/1731